YOUR KNOWLEDGE HAS VALUE

- We will publish your bachelor's and master's thesis, essays and papers

- Your own eBook and book - sold worldwide in all relevant shops

- Earn money with each sale

Upload your text at www.GRIN.com
and publish for free

Geo-Environmental Political Adaptation

Hafiz Abdul Hamid Salifu

Bibliographic information published by the German National Library:

The German National Library lists this publication in the National Bibliography; detailed bibliographic data are available on the Internet at http://dnb.dnb.de.

ISBN: 9783389064481
This book is also available as an ebook.

Inhaltsverzeichnis

1. Introduction

1.1 Background and Context

The relationship between environmental conditions and societal development has been a central theme in geographical and political studies. Environmental determinism posits that geographic and climatic factors exert profound influences on human societies, shaping their cultural practices, economic activities, and political structures (Diamond, 1997; Huntington, 1996). This theory becomes particularly significant when applied to Africa, a continent marked by diverse ecological landscapes ranging from the Sahara Desert in the north to the Congo rainforest in the central region and the savannas of the south. Each of these regions imposes distinct challenges and opportunities for governance and resource management.

Africa's political history has been shaped not only by its indigenous governance systems but also by external influences, most notably the imposition of Western political ideologies during the colonial period (Mamdani, 1996; Young, 1994). The introduction of these ideologies often disregarded local environmental contexts and cultural practices, resulting in governance structures ill-suited to Africa's unique environmental realities. This historical legacy continues to impact governance effectiveness and stability in many African countries today (Mamdani, 1996).

1.2 Motivation for GEPA

The motivation behind Geo-Environmental Political Adaptation (GEPA) lies in addressing these historical and contemporary challenges. GEPA proposes a theoretical framework that integrates environmental determinism into the development of political ideologies and governance structures in Africa. By emphasizing the adaptation of governance models to local geographic and climatic conditions, GEPA seeks to foster political stability, enhance governance effectiveness, and promote sustainable development across the continent.

1.3 Objective of the Paper

This paper aims to introduce and elucidate the Geo-Environmental Political Adaptation (GEPA) theory within the academic disciplines of Geography and Political Science. Specifically, it seeks to achieve the following objectives:

- Define and Elaborate on GEPA: Provide a comprehensive definition of GEPA and outline its components, emphasizing its integration of environmental determinism with political ideologies tailored to African contexts.

- Explore Empirical Evidence and Case Studies: Examine empirical evidence and case studies that support the core propositions of GEPA, including how environmental factors influence political structures, resource management practices, and governance stability in different African regions.

- Discuss Policy Implications and Governance Reforms: Analyze the policy implications derived from GEPA and propose governance reforms aimed at aligning political systems with environmental realities. Offer recommendations for policymakers, international organizations, and local communities to enhance resilience and sustainability in African governance frameworks.

By critically examining the intersections of environmental determinism, political ideologies, and governance structures in Africa through the lens of GEPA, this paper contributes to a deeper understanding of how environmental factors shape political outcomes and governance practices on the continent. It underscores the importance of context-specific approaches to governance that acknowledge and integrate environmental considerations, thereby promoting more effective and sustainable development pathways for Africa.

2. Theoretical Framework: Geo-Environmental Political Adaptation (GEPA)

2.1 Definition and Components of GEPA

Geo-Environmental Political Adaptation (GEPA) represents a novel theoretical framework that integrates environmental determinism with the development of political ideologies and governance structures in Africa. At its core, GEPA asserts that geographic and climatic factors play a pivotal role in shaping societal organization and governance practices (Diamond, 1997; Huntington, 1996). By acknowledging and adapting to these environmental realities, GEPA aims to enhance political stability, improve governance effectiveness, and foster sustainable development across the continent.

The components of GEPA encompass several key elements:

- Integration of Environmental Determinism: GEPA emphasizes the influence of environmental conditions, such as terrain, climate variability, and natural resource distribution, on political structures and decision-making processes. For instance, regions prone to arid climates or water scarcity may necessitate centralized governance to manage and allocate limited resources effectively (Mamdani, 1996).

- Adaptation of Political Ideologies: Unlike one-size-fits-all approaches, GEPA advocates for adaptive political ideologies that are responsive to local environmental contexts. This adaptation involves tailoring governance models to accommodate the ecological diversity and socio-economic dynamics present in various African regions (Young, 1994).

- Sustainability and Resilience: Central to GEPA is the promotion of sustainable governance practices that ensure the long-term viability of natural resources and socio-

4

economic systems. By aligning political frameworks with environmental realities, GEPA seeks to mitigate environmental degradation and enhance community resilience against climate change impacts (Diamond, 1997).

2.2 Literature Review

The theoretical underpinnings of GEPA draw upon a diverse body of literature spanning Geography, Political Science, Environmental Studies, and African Studies. Key scholarly works that inform and support GEPA include:

•　Environmental Determinism: Scholars like Jared Diamond and Samuel Huntington have explored how geographic and environmental factors influence societal development and political outcomes. Diamond's seminal work, Guns, Germs, and Steel, highlights how environmental conditions shape historical patterns of civilization and governance (Diamond, 1997). Huntington's Clash of Civilizations theory examines how cultural and environmental differences contribute to global conflicts and governance challenges (Huntington, 1996).

•　Colonial Legacy and Governance: Mahmood Mamdani's Citizen and Subject critiques the imposition of Western political ideologies during colonialism and its enduring impacts on African governance systems (Mamdani, 1996). Mamdani argues that colonial powers often imposed governance models that disregarded local environmental contexts and cultural practices, leading to institutional inefficiencies and social unrest.

•　Adaptive Governance Models: Charles Young's comparative study on African colonial states underscores the importance of adaptive governance models that blend indigenous practices with modern administrative structures (Young, 1994). Young's research highlights successful cases where African countries have integrated traditional governance systems with contemporary environmental policies to address local challenges effectively.

2.3 The Significance of GEPA in African Contexts

GEPA addresses significant gaps in current governance theories by foregrounding environmental determinism as a critical factor in shaping political ideologies and governance structures in Africa. The framework challenges the universal applicability of Western political models and advocates for context-specific approaches that acknowledge and integrate environmental realities.

By synthesizing insights from environmental determinism, colonial history, and adaptive governance practices, GEPA offers a robust framework for policymakers, researchers, and practitioners seeking to promote sustainable development and governance stability in Africa. This theoretical approach not only enriches academic discourse but also provides practical guidance for addressing contemporary governance challenges in a rapidly changing global environment.

3. Core Propositions of GEPA

Geo-Environmental Political Adaptation (GEPA) posits several core propositions that elucidate how environmental determinism intersects with political ideologies and governance structures in Africa. These propositions highlight the influence of geographic and climatic factors on governance needs, the legacy of colonial interventions, and the repercussions of mismatches between Western models and African realities.

3.1 Environmental Influences on Political Structures

GEPA underscores the profound impact of environmental conditions on shaping political structures and governance practices across Africa. Geographic factors such as terrain, climate variability, and natural resource distribution significantly influence societal organization and resource management strategies (Diamond, 1997; Huntington, 1996). For instance, regions characterized by arid climates or limited water resources may necessitate centralized governance to ensure equitable resource allocation and mitigate conflicts over scarce resources (Mamdani, 1996).

Moreover, environmental conditions dictate economic activities and livelihood strategies, thereby influencing the social dynamics and political demands within communities. In regions with abundant natural resources, decentralized governance models may promote local autonomy and resource management practices tailored to community needs (Young, 1994).

3.2 Historical and Colonial Legacies

The imposition of Western political ideologies during the colonial era has left enduring legacies on African governance systems. Colonial powers often implemented governance structures that disregarded local environmental contexts and cultural practices, aiming to consolidate control and exploit natural resources for economic gain (Mamdani, 1996). This historical legacy has contributed to institutional inefficiencies, social inequalities, and conflicts over resource management in post-colonial Africa.

GEPA critically examines how these historical interventions continue to shape contemporary governance challenges, emphasizing the need to decolonize African political systems by integrating indigenous knowledge and environmental considerations into governance reforms (Mamdani, 1996; Young, 1994).

3.3 Mismatch Between Western Models and African Realities

A central tenet of GEPA is the recognition that Western political models, developed in different environmental and cultural contexts, often fail to address the complexities of African realities. The adoption of Western ideologies without adaptation to local environmental conditions can lead to governance inefficiencies, social unrest, and environmental degradation (Diamond, 1997; Huntington, 1996).

For example, attempts to implement Western-style democracy in contexts where geographic and climatic factors hinder access to education and infrastructure may exacerbate inequalities and undermine governance legitimacy (Mamdani, 1996). GEPA advocates for context-specific approaches that blend indigenous governance practices with modern administrative structures, thereby enhancing governance effectiveness and promoting sustainable development in Africa (Young, 1994).

Conclusion

In summary, Geo-Environmental Political Adaptation (GEPA) advances several core propositions that highlight the interplay between environmental determinism, political ideologies, and governance structures in Africa. By acknowledging the influence of geographic and climatic factors, addressing colonial legacies, and critiquing mismatches between Western models and African realities, GEPA offers a comprehensive framework for understanding and reforming governance practices on the continent. The next section will explore empirical evidence and case studies that support these propositions, demonstrating how GEPA can inform policy development and governance reforms in diverse African contexts.

4. Hypotheses and Empirical Analysis

Geo-Environmental Political Adaptation (GEPA) posits several hypotheses that explore how environmental determinism influences political structures, governance effectiveness, and stability in Africa. This section presents empirical evidence and case studies to support these hypotheses, demonstrating the practical applicability of GEPA in understanding and addressing governance challenges across the continent.

4.1 H1: Centralized Governance in Regions with Environmental Challenges

GEPA hypothesizes that regions facing severe environmental challenges, such as arid climates or water scarcity, exhibit more centralized governance structures. Centralization may be necessary to coordinate resource management, ensure equitable distribution of scarce resources, and mitigate conflicts over land and water resources (Mamdani, 1996; Huntington, 1996).

Empirical Evidence: Case studies from arid regions in Africa, such as the Sahel and Horn of Africa, illustrate how centralized governance frameworks have been implemented to manage water resources and address desertification. Countries like Ethiopia and Niger have established centralized water management systems to regulate irrigation and mitigate drought impacts, thereby promoting agricultural sustainability and social stability (Mamdani, 1996).

4.2 H2: Integration of Traditional Governance with Environmental Adaptation

GEPA suggests that African countries integrating traditional governance structures with modern environmental adaptation strategies experience greater political stability and governance effectiveness. Traditional governance systems often embody community-based

9

resource management practices that are well-adapted to local environmental conditions (Young, 1994).

Empirical Evidence: Studies from countries like Botswana and Namibia highlight successful examples of integrating indigenous knowledge systems with contemporary environmental policies. These countries have implemented community-based natural resource management initiatives, such as communal conservancies and wildlife management areas, which enhance local participation, promote conservation efforts, and improve livelihoods (Young, 1994).

4.3 H3: Impact of Western Political Ideologies on African Governance

GEPA examines how the imposition of Western political ideologies without adaptation to local environmental realities can lead to governance challenges and instability in Africa. Western models of democracy, for example, may face challenges in contexts where geographic and climatic factors hinder infrastructure development and access to education (Diamond, 1997).

Empirical Evidence: Instances of political instability and governance crises in African countries often coincide with attempts to transplant Western democratic institutions without addressing underlying environmental constraints. Countries experiencing rapid urbanization and population growth, coupled with environmental degradation, frequently struggle with governance inefficiencies and social unrest (Diamond, 1997).

Conclusion

In conclusion, Geo-Environmental Political Adaptation (GEPA) presents hypotheses that highlight the nuanced relationships between environmental determinism, political ideologies, and governance outcomes in Africa. Through empirical analysis and case studies, GEPA provides insights into how adaptive governance strategies can enhance political stability, improve governance effectiveness, and promote sustainable development across diverse African contexts. The following section will explore policy implications and governance reforms derived from GEPA, offering recommendations for policymakers, practitioners, and researchers to address contemporary challenges and foster resilience in African governance frameworks.

5. Implications for Policy and Governance

Geo-Environmental Political Adaptation (GEPA) offers significant implications for policy development and governance reforms in Africa, advocating for context-specific approaches that integrate environmental determinism into political ideologies and governance structures. This section explores the practical implications of GEPA, providing recommendations for policymakers, stakeholders, and researchers to promote sustainable development, enhance governance effectiveness, and foster resilience in African governance frameworks.

5.1 Policy Development

GEPA underscores the importance of integrating environmental considerations into policy development processes. Policymakers should prioritize the formulation of governance frameworks that are resilient to environmental challenges and capable of managing natural resources sustainably. This involves:

- **Environmental Impact Assessments:** Conducting comprehensive environmental impact assessments (EIAs) to evaluate the potential consequences of policy decisions on natural ecosystems and local communities.

- Adaptive Management Strategies: Implementing adaptive management strategies that allow for flexible adjustments in response to changing environmental conditions, such as climate variability and resource depletion.

- Community Engagement and Participation: Fostering meaningful engagement with local communities and indigenous groups in policy formulation processes to ensure inclusive decision-making and sustainable development outcomes.

5.2 Governance Reforms

GEPA advocates for governance reforms that blend Western political ideologies with traditional African governance structures adapted to local environmental realities. Key reforms include:

- Decentralized Governance: Promoting decentralized governance models that empower local communities to manage natural resources and address environmental challenges effectively.

- Integration of Indigenous Knowledge: Incorporating indigenous knowledge systems and customary laws into formal governance frameworks to enhance resource management practices and promote cultural preservation.

- Capacity Building and Institutional Strengthening: Investing in capacity building programs and institutional strengthening initiatives to build resilience in governance institutions and improve service delivery in remote and environmentally vulnerable regions.

5.3 Further Research

While GEPA offers valuable insights into the intersections of environmental determinism and political ideologies in Africa, further research is essential to deepen understanding and inform evidence-based policy interventions. Areas for further exploration include:

- Comparative Studies: Conducting comparative studies across different African regions to assess the effectiveness of adaptive governance strategies in addressing environmental challenges and promoting socio-economic development.

- Longitudinal Analysis: Undertaking longitudinal analysis to track the evolution of governance systems in response to changing environmental conditions and external pressures.

- Policy Evaluation and Impact Assessment: Evaluating the impact of policy interventions informed by GEPA on governance outcomes, environmental sustainability, and community resilience over time.

Conclusion

In conclusion, Geo-Environmental Political Adaptation (GEPA) provides a robust framework for policymakers, practitioners, and researchers to address contemporary governance challenges in Africa. By integrating environmental determinism into political ideologies and governance structures, GEPA promotes sustainable development, enhances governance effectiveness, and fosters resilience in the face of environmental uncertainties. The recommendations outlined in this section offer practical pathways for advancing adaptive governance reforms and ensuring inclusive, environmentally sustainable development across the continent.

Reference

❖ Diamond, J. (1997). Guns, Germs, and Steel: The Fates of Human Societies. New York: W. W. Norton & Company.

❖ Huntington, S. P. (1996). The Clash of Civilizations and the Remaking of World Order. New York: Simon & Schuster.

❖ Mamdani, M. (1996). Citizen and Subject: Contemporary Africa and the Legacy of Late Colonialism. Princeton, NJ: Princeton University Press.

❖ Young, C. (1994). The African Colonial State in Comparative Perspective. New Haven, CT: Yale University Press.

❖ Mamdani, M. (1996). "Beyond Settler and Native as Political Identities: Overcoming the Political Legacy of Colonialism," in Citizen and Subject: Contemporary Africa and the Legacy of Late Colonialism. Princeton, NJ: Princeton University Press, pp. 25-60.

❖ Diamond, J. (1999). "The Third Chimpanzee: The Evolution and Future of the Human Animal." New York: Harper Collins.

❖ Huntington, S. P. (1993). "The Clash of Civilizations?" Foreign Affairs, 72(3), 22-49.

❖ Young, C. (1995). "African Conflicts and Informal Power: Big Men and Networks." Review of African Political Economy, 22(65), 355-372.

❖ UNDP. (2019). "Human Development Report 2019: Beyond Income, Beyond Averages, Beyond Today - Inequalities in Human Development in the 21st Century." New York: United Nations Development Programme.

❖ World Bank. (2018). "Africa's Cities: Opening Doors to the World." Washington, DC: World Bank.

YOUR KNOWLEDGE HAS VALUE